Florian Kurtz

IT-Architecture as Enabler of Business Processes

GRIN Publishing

Bibliographic information published by the German National Library:

The German National Library lists this publication in the National Bibliography; detailed bibliographic data are available on the Internet at http://dnb.dnb.de .

Imprint:

Copyright © 2011 GRIN Verlag GmbH
Print and binding: Books on Demand GmbH, Norderstedt Germany
ISBN: 978-3-656-08171-5

This book at GRIN:

http://www.grin.com/en/e-book/183570/it-architecture-as-enabler-of-business-processes

GRIN - Your knowledge has value

Since its foundation in 1998, GRIN has specialized in publishing academic texts by students, college teachers and other academics as e-book and printed book. The website www.grin.com is an ideal platform for presenting term papers, final papers, scientific essays, dissertations and specialist books.

Visit us on the internet:

http://www.grin.com/

http://www.facebook.com/grincom

http://www.twitter.com/grin_com

IT-Architecture as Enabler of Business Processes

Assignment

Enterprise and IT-Architecture management

Due Date

21 November 2011

Table of contents

Table of figures

List of abbreviations

Cf.   Confer

N.u.   Name unknown

SOA   Service-oriented architecture

IT   Information and telecommunication

1 Introduction

For many companies the incorporating of their business processes into the existing IT-Landscape becomes a great challenge. In the majority of cases the existing models for business processes were developed by non-technical business analysts, who do not usually consider the limitations, concurrency, granularity or interaction models of the existing IT-Landscape.

In times of dynamically changing markets and the progressive motion towards globalization in companies, it is increasingly important for companies to adapt their IT-Landscape and business processes to changing conditions.

For this reason, this assignment will provide an overview of the importance the IT-Architecture, which enables and supports business processes. In addition it will give an insight to the service oriented architecture and it's meaning in this context.

The main target of this assignment is to explain which technologies are available to adapt the IT-Landscape to dynamically changing requirements in companies and how IT-Architecture enables business processes to respond to these changing requirements.

2 Definitions

In this chapter the basic definitions are given, to get a common understanding of the terminology, which is used in this assignment.

2.1 IT-Architecture

To define what an IT-Architecture is, the ISO/IEC 42010-2007 (Systems and software engineering – Architecture description) tells us it is:

„The fundamental organization of a system, embodied in its components, their relationships to each other an the environment, and the principles governing its design and evolution. Practically it is represented in architectural descriptions from the viewpoints of the stakeholders."[1]

So an IT-Architecture based on this definition is a framework, which describes the structure of an IT-System and its interfaces to other software components in a company. These interfaces can be to other IT-Systems but also to business processes. If an IT-Architecture describes interfaces to the business processes of a company, we can say that this IT-Architecture enables business processes.

2.2 Business Process

Business processes are essential to understand how companies operate. They play an important role in the realization of flexible IT-Systems, and consequently also for IT-Architecture. This assignment deals with business processes. There are many definitions for business processes. For this assignment I will use the following definition:

---

[1] Schönbächler, M. et al., 2011, p. 15

„A business process consists of a set of activities that are performed in coordination in an organizational and technical environment. These activities jointly realize a business goal. Each business process is enacted by a single organization, but it may interact with business processes performed by other organizations."[2]

Based on this definition, we can see that companies interact with business partners to construct a network. This is why it is necessary that a company's IT-Architecture enables business processes beyond corporate limits.

2.3 Enterprise IT-Architecture

If an IT-Architecture supports or enables the business processes of a company, it is called enterprise IT-Architecture. So we can define enterprise IT-Architecture as follows:

„Enterprise IT-Architecture is the organizing logic for business processes and its in-frastructure"[3]

Taking this definition further, we can see that the topic of IT-Architecture as enabler of business processes is not new. However the still unresolved problem is the flexible implementation of an IT-Architecture and the degree of support for business processes. In the most companies there is still great potential for improvement in these areas.

---

[2] Weske, M., 2007, p. 5
[3] Perks et al., 2003, C., p. 341

3 IT-Architecture

This chapter gives an overview of IT-Architecture. It explains the structure and the individual components of an IT-Architecture. Furthermore, we will see the different influential factors an IT-Architecture must react to.

In the last section of this chapter will show how IT-Architecture can support or enable business processes.

3.1 Influential factors to IT-Architecture

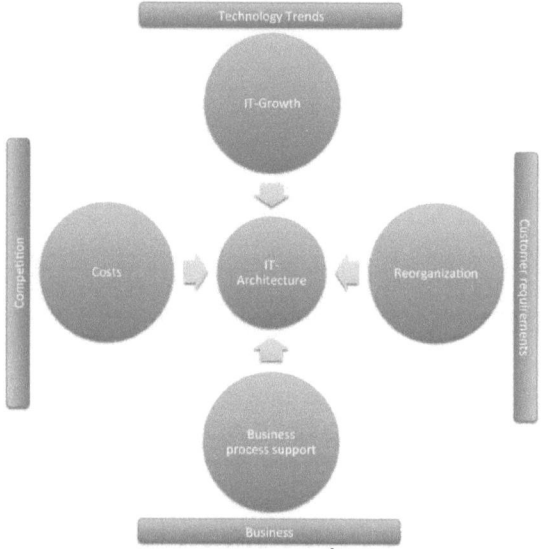

Figure 1: Factors influencing IT-Architecture[4]

Figure 1 represents the major factors, which influence the IT-Architecture. We can see that the IT-Architecture has to react to many dynamically changing factors. These factors are technology trends, customer requirements, competition and the business. The business should be treated as the main influential factor for the IT-Architecture; however, because, when an IT-Architecture supports the business

---

[4] Own representation according to N.u. 2011

process in a optimal way it can provide a major competitive advantage for a company. Related to this advantage, the value creation can be increased.[5]

Of course, the other factors should not be neglected, but this assignment concentrates on the business factor.

3.2 Structure of IT-Architecture

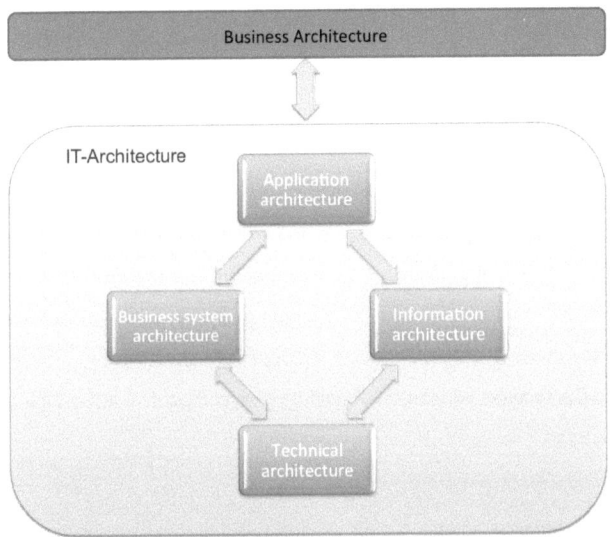

Figure 2: IT-Architecture components[6]

In figure 2 we see that the IT-Architecture consist of many architectural disciplines. Each of these sub architectures stand in interaction with each other.

This interaction works both ways: On the one hand, to design an IT-Architecture that enables business processes, it is necessary that the business architecture sets requirements for the conception of the IT-Architecture. On the other hand, the business architecture has to include the possibilities and restrictions of the IT-Architecture.

---

[5] cf. N.u. 2011
[6] Own representation

The different components of an IT-Architecture are shown more detailed in the chapters below.

3.2.1 Application architecture

The application architecture, also known as software architecture, defines the structures of individual systems based on defined technology.[7]

In the selection of a software technology it is very important to evaluate the different possibilities and choose a technology that supports the organizational needs and the business processes as well as possible.

3.2.2 Information architecture

An information architecture defines the design of the provision of information within an organization. It's very important for an organization that the correct information or data is delivered at the right time to the right place.[8]

Information architecture is necessary, because, an organization, which can provide the information to the receiver very quickly, could be a big competitive advantage.

3.2.3 Business system architecture

The business system architecture sketches in which way the software systems of an organization can be structured to effectively pursue its business objectives. So business system architecture gives an overview of how the IT-Systems supports the business processes and how it defines the interfaces between them.[9]

3.2.4 Technical architecture

---

[7] cf. Perks et al., 2003, C., p. 4
[8] cf. Wagter, R. et al, 2005, p.39
[9] cf. Wagter, R. et al, 2005, p.39

The technical architecture defines the technical environment and infrastructure in which all information systems exist.[10]

This part of the architecture sketches in which way IT-Hardware must be deployed to get a fast and low cost IT-Infrastructure. With respect to the given question, however, this architecture can be neglected, because, the technical architecture enables the software which is running on it, but not the business processes directly.

3.3 From IT-Architecture to Enterprise Architecture

When an IT-Architecture and business architecture work together we call it enterprise architecture. How do we come from a sepearted IT- and business architecture to a common one? This requires an IT-Allignment.

An IT-Allignment describes the way organizations can make IT and business conform to one another. However, it is not only strategical, it is also an operational process between business and IT. The IT-Allignemnt includes the linking between the business and the IT-Architecture.

It also makes satements about the degree of cooperation between business processes and the IT-Architecture. Therefore the IT-Allignemnt is very important in order to get a consensus between these two architectures.[11]

---

[10] cf. Perks et al., 2003, C., p. 4
[11] cf., Linthicum D. S., 2003, p.29

4 IT-Architecture and business processes

4.1 Enterprise Application Integration

Enterprise application integration (EAI) is a model to connect different applications to each other along a business process. This connection between the applications makes complex business processes possible.

EAI is defined in the computerworld from 4th October as follows:

"Enterprise application integration involves linking applications, whether purchased or developed in-house, so they can better support a business process. Although there are myriad vendors that offer a variety of approaches, most packaged EAI software will offer users tools to model their business processes and link the applications with middleware that can make each application communicate via data messages."[12]

Based on this definition of EAI and the model that the individual software components communicate via messages with each other, the EAI can be seen as predecessor for the service oriented architecture (SOA). To the concerning difference between EAI and SOA all software components persist as before., but in a service oriented architecture all software components are realized as services.

4.2 Service oriented Architecture

Nowadays, when anyone speaks about business processes and IT-Architecture, the buzzword is service-oriented architecture (SOA). The reason for this is that SOA gives the promise to minimize the IT costs and to fit to the business processes better. One definition would be that:

---

[12] N.u. 1999, p.72

"A service-oriented Architecture is a framework for integrating business processes and supporting IT-Infrastructure as secure, standardized components – services – that can be reused and combined to address changing business priorities."[13]

The speciality of a service-oriented architecture is that all software components are realized in services. Any of these services can be replaced by each other. Consequently, companies with an SOA are very flexible in changing their business processes and reacting to the market requests. This is shown in figure 3.

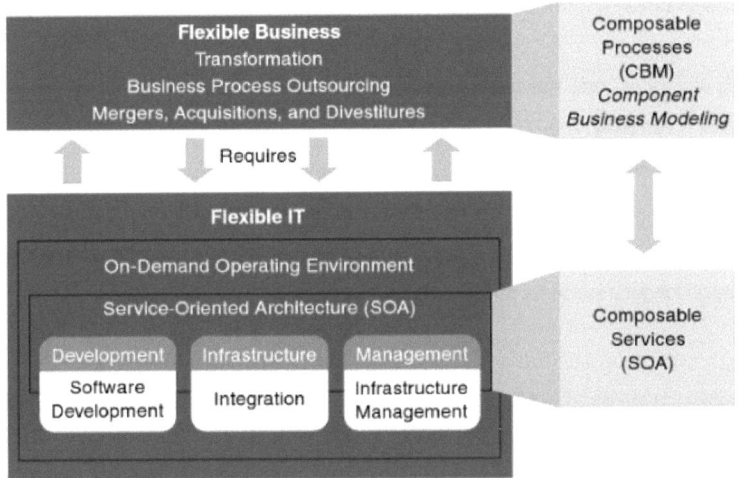

Figure 3: SOA and business processes[14]

Considereding the fact of increasing globalization and the growing price pressure, SOA has another advantage for organizations. Services of an SOA can not only be used within an organization over the intranet, rhey can also be used from organizations all over the world via the internet.

---

[13] Bieberstein, N. et al., 2008, p. 4
[14] Gurugé, A., 2004, p. 19

Based on this advantage, organizations can outsource their business processes to countries where the production is cheaper, or they can connect their business locations in order to collaborate more efficiently.

4.2.1 WebServices

WebServices are an expression of a SOA. WebServices consits of several open standards, which realize a service-oriented architecture. In figure 4 an example is given, illustrating how WebServices can support or enable new market-oriented business processes, using the example of a travel portal.

This illustrates, that the business process for hotel bookings must not be longer within a company. A business process, which is realized with WebServices may extend over many companies.

This has the advantage that the travel firm can concentrate on its core business – to book hotels and flights. Other operations like exchange rates or offer validations they no longer need to be taken care of.

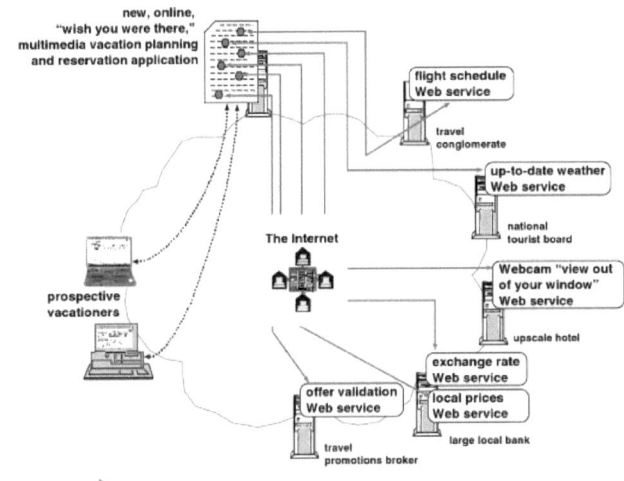

Figure 4: Business process across distributed Systsems with Web Services[15]

An SOA with WebServices provides a very flexible architecture that supports business processes. In addition, this architecture enables business processes which were previously not possible., because, new business processes are conceivable across corporate borders.

So, in this case, IT-Architecture is an enabler of business processes.

---

[15] Bose, S., 2005, p. 3

5 Resume and perspective

Retrospective it can be said that IT-Architecture as an enabler of business processes is a much discussed topic. In times of dynamically changing markets and high competition pressure, it is very important for an organization to be flexible.
This flexibility can only be achieved with the support of the existing IT-Systems. Without this support, organizations lose a very important competition factor; because, they need a very long time to react to new requirements.

Further, value creating business processes are the only processes in an organization, which bring money in. If these processes are optimally supported by the IT, the enterprise value is much higher than that of the competitors.

Looking ahead, IT-Architecture and the enablement or support of business processes is constantly in development. Because, on the one hand new IT trends bring new IT possibilities with them, on the other hand, the products and consequently the business processes become more complex and must be modified.

SOA and WebServices are an approach to react to dynamically changing and high-pressure markets. They give companies the flexibility, which is needed. They support and enable business processes in a very efficient way. In future the development for IT-Architectures will continue and will bring new IT-Architecture models, which adapt to business processes in a better way than IT-Architectures do today. At the moment, an SOA with WebServices is the best way to realize and enable new business processes, in my opinion.

List of references

Bieberstein, Norbert; Laird, Robert G.; Dr. Jones, Keith; Mitra, Tilak; (2008): Executing SOA – A practical Guide for the Service-Oriented Architect. 1st Edition Boston: IBM Press.

Bose, Sanjay; Bieberstein, Norbert, Fiammante, Marc, Jones, Keith, Shah, Rawn; (2005): Service-oriented architecture compass – business value, olanning and enterprise roadmap. 1st Edition New Jersey: Pearson Educa

Gurugé, Anura; (2004): Web services - theory and practice. 1st Edition Oxford: Elsevier Digital Press.

Linthicum, David S.; (2003): Enterprise Architektur Management. 5th Edition New Jersey: Addison-Wesley.

N.u. (2011): IT-Architekturen richtig strukturieren. From: http://www.cio.de/strategien/analysen/811701/. Print date: 13.11.2011.

Perks, Col; Beveridge, Tony; (2003): Guide to Enterprise IT-Architecture. 1st Edition New York: Springer Verlag.

Schönbächler, Markus; Pfiste, Cuno (2011): IT-Architektur – Grundlagen, Konzepte und Umsetzung. 1st Edition Münster: Verlagshaus Monsenstein und Vannerdat.

Wagter, Roel; van den Berg, Martin; Luijpers, Joost; van Steenbergen, Marlies; (2005): Dynamic Enterprise Architecture – How to make it work. 1st Edition New Jersey: John Wiley & Sons.

Weske, Matthias; (2007): Business Process Management – Concepts, Languages, Architectures. 1st Edition Heidelberg: Springer Verlag.